WORKSHOP MODELS FOR FAMILY LIFE EDUCATION

COUPLES COMMUNICATION
AND
NEGOTIATION SKILLS

Diana Richmond Garland

Family Service Association of America
44 East 23rd Street
New York, New York 10010

Copyright © 1978 by
Family Service Association of America
44 East 23rd Street, New York, New York 10010

All rights reserved. No part of this book may be reproduced or transmitted in any form or by any means, electronic or mechanical, including photocopying, recording, or by any information storage and retrieval system, without permission in writing from the publisher.

Library of Congress Cataloging in Publication Data

Garland, Diana Richmond, 1950-
    Couples communication and negotiation skills.

    (Workshop models for family life education)
    Bibliography: p. 121
    1. Marriage counseling--United States. 2. Family life education--Study and teaching--United States.
3. Family social work--United States.
4. Interpersonal communication. 5. Group relations training. I. Title. II. Series.
HQ10.G373   362.8'2   77-26981
ISBN 0-87304-158-5

Final manuscript typed by Dolores Matarazzo.

Printed in the U.S.A.

PREFACE

<u>Workshop Models for Family Life Education</u> is a series of manuals intended to promote the exploration of new alternatives and the utilization of new options in day-to-day living through programs in family life education.

Basically, family life education is a service of planned intervention that applies the dynamic process of group learning to improving the quality of individual and family living. The manuals are in workshop format and offer possible new approaches of service to families. They are meant to serve as a training mechanism and basic framework for group leaders involved in FLE workshops.

In 1974, the Family Service Association of America appointed a National Task Force on Family Life Education, Development, and Enrichment. One of the goals of the Task Force was to assess the importance and future direction of family life education services within family service agencies. One of the recommendations of their report was to "recognize family life education, development, and enrichment as one of the three major services of the family service agency: family counseling, family life education, and family advocacy."[1] This recommendation was adopted by the Board of Directors of FSAA and has become basic policy of the Association.

---

1. "Overview of Findings of the FSAA Task Force on Family Life Education, Development, and Enrichment" (New York: Family Service Association of America, May 1976), p. 21 (mimeographed).

An interest in family life education is a natural development of FSAA's role in the strengthening of family life and complementary to the more traditional remedial functions of family agencies. FLE programs can add a new dimension to the services provided by family agencies. They can open an agency to the general population by providing programs which are appropriate for all families and individuals, not only for those at risk. They provide a new arena for service that deals with growth as well as dysfunction. They can encourage agencies to look beyond the therapeutic approach and to take on a new objective for the enrichment and strengthening of family life. For the participants, FLE programs can lead to increased understanding of normal stress, growth of esteem for one's self and others, development of communications skills, improved ability to cope with problem situations, development of problem-solving skills, and maximization of family and individual potential.

This series provides tangible evidence of FSAA's continuing interest in family life education and of a belief in its future importance for family services. FLE programs, coordinated within a total agency program and viewed as a vital and integral part of the agency, can become key factors in family service concern for growth and development within all families.

W. Keith Daugherty
General Director
Family Service Association
of America

TABLE OF CONTENTS

PREFACE	iii
FOREWORD	1
INTRODUCTION	5
SESSION 1	
Brief Outline	15
Role Plays and Exercises	
"A Person Cannot not Communicate"	21
Nonverbal Communication	22
Development of Guidelines for Communication	23
Preworkshop Questionnaire	29
Handouts	35
SESSION 2	
Brief Outline	47
Role Plays and Exercises	
Paraphrasing	51
Observing and Attending Skills	55
Reaching for Information	58
Handouts	67
SESSION 3	
Brief Outline	71
Role Plays and Exercises	
Pinpointing the Question	75
Staying on the Issue	77
Determination of Fact or Opinion	82
Handouts	89

SESSION 4
    Brief Outline   95
    Role Plays and Exercises
        Matters of Fact   99
        Matters of Opinion   101
    Handouts   107

POSTWORKSHOP QUESTIONNAIRE   113
BIBLIOGRAPHY   121

FOREWORD

This manual is aimed toward those social workers and other group leaders who want to offer short-term task-focused programs to couples interested in enhancing their marriages. In several respects, this trainer's guide is a unique addition to the literature dealing with family functioning. It concerns "every family," because it aims to bring alive such basic values as respect for one's own world view as well as those of others, openness in communication, and spontaneity in relationships. Who among us does not cherish such goals?

The thrust is optimistic and specific. The approach suggests that couples--especially those new, young couples whose patterns of interaction have not yet become encrusted and rigid--can be taught specific skills. A key assumption here is that these teachable/learnable skills can be used in a variety of ways to produce changing, open, growing family communication systems.

The Couples Communication and Negotiation Workshop forms an integral part of family life education and stands as an additional alternative to the more traditional family services that hinge upon therapy, counseling, or lecturing. Thus, its target population is broad, for it can be offered wherever families naturally come together. Such workshops should be a component of outreach programs sponsored through various community auspices--schools, churches, community centers, libraries--as well as by the family service agency at its home quarters.

The material offered in the workshop is educational in the finest sense of adult education methodology. The participants are viewed as "normals"--as learners, not as patients, clients, or cases. The sessions are experiential and carefully sequenced to involve the whole person--the thinking, feeling, and behaving person. Although the major desired outcome is changed, self-controlled behavior, the content encompasses ideas, information, values, and feelings as well as behavior. All are necessary learnings that will affect how one acts or behaves. There is a linkage here with the tradition in social work and education that views the individual holistically as a complex entity with consciousness, purpose, and self that must be acknowledged along with the behavior.

Workshops growing out of this framework will not focus upon families caught up in pathological struggles nor riddled by hidden agendas. They will deal with the common shared problems with which most families struggle, especially those inherent in the closeness/separateness dilemma that confounds all intimate relationships. Couples and families are helped through this framework to create their own unique interactional patterns as they become more skilled in managing the delicate balance that is part of the everyday strain of living in close quarters with another person.

Guidelines are offered the group leader (or leaders) to show couples where they stand at the beginning and one month after the conclusion of the sessions and to present the selected learning experiences with ample detail of precise content, activities, and practice opportunities for learning and enacting the ten basic skills that form the heart of the approach. In this sense the manual is a how-to-do-it manual for the group leader with considerable attention devoted to the details of structuring and presenting material that would be encouraging to the novice as well as the experienced group leader.

There are three components to this four-session (ten-hour) couples communication workshop manual. In the Introduction the theoretical basis for the content focus of the workshop (enhanced communication and negotiation skills) and the theoretical basis for the teaching approach are elaborated. The middle section contains a step-by-step discussion of the four workshop sessions, specific pre- and post-workshop questionnaires, the behavioral observation rating scales used during the sessions, and other specific instructional materials that are part of the sessions. The manual concludes with the bibliographical references used in designing the material.

This manual can be used or modified to suit special circumstances by imaginative, innovative social workers and others to present a lively learning challenge to the many couples who will want to use their group experience to learn to communicate and resolve differences of opinion more effectively.

September 1977   Ruth R. Middleman
                                                          University of Louisville
                                                          Louisville, Kentucky

INTRODUCTION

There has been a flurry of activity in recent years based on the assumption that, for one reason or another, the institution of marriage is somehow failing. Treatment approaches of all shapes and sizes have emerged out of concern for doing something about "dysfunctional" marriages. Comparatively speaking, however, there have been few studies of the characteristics of healthy family and marital systems. Jerry M. Lewis et al., in one of the available studies, pinpointed this problem in their statement that "we, like most mental health professionals, have limited sources of information regarding families, deriving data from our own families of origin, our current families, and uncertain extrapolations from clinical work with dysfunctional families."[1] One wonders, then, what our goals have been in therapy, because health has really never been defined with a substantial basis in research.

If there has been little study of healthy family and marital systems, there has been even less concern on the part of mental health professionals with providing for the development of healthy family systems through education and socialization processes aimed at preventing later problems. This would seem to be a fruitful area in which to direct more effort in attempts to develop alternatives to the remedial approach of therapy which now predominates in the mental health field. This is much the same conclusion which Lewis et al. reached:

---

1. Jerry M. Lewis, W. Robert Beavers, John T. Gossett, and Virginia Austin Phillips, No Single Thread (New York: Brunner/Mazel, 1976).

> As data develop regarding the roles social structures play in individual emotional illness, the thrust of professional efforts can be directed toward ways to avert such dysfunction. The family, young families especially, is a logical focus. In a useful analogy, young families may be likened to an infant. The family as an organism undergoes a series of developmental sequences. Over time, a family's characteristic style of reacting may become increasingly "fixed." Young families, therefore, are reasonably unencumbered by family developmental events and may represent organisms unusually responsive to education.[2]

This workshop is concerned with teaching skills which will enable young couples to develop changing, open, growing family communication systems. It should be emphasized that this is not therapy--it is skills training. Nor is it an appropriate substitute for therapy. Neither should it be considered an attempt to provide all the skills which are, or could be helpful in developing a healthy family/marital system. The concern is with one aspect of the marital system--verbal interaction as it occurs in communication and negotiating conflict-- and, even at that, the focus has been narrowed to encompass a few specific skills.

The theoretical bases for the selection of the specific skills included in this workshop are the findings of Lewis et al. in their study of healthy families. Three of the eight characteristics which they describe for optimal families have formed the basis for the development of these skills: (1) a respect for one's own and the subjective world view of others; (2) openness in communication versus distancing, obscuring, and confusing mechanisms; and (3) spontaneity versus rigid stereotyped interactions. As one examines the skills which this work-

---

2. Ibid., pp. 4-5.

shop emphasizes, their foundation on the premises of the first two characteristics is obvious. The third characteristic was not the basis for the direct formulation of any specific skill, but rather served as a guideline by which to examine the goals of the workshop. There has been a concerted attempt to steer away from any step-by-step formulation of how couples should communicate, as is so evident in many treatment modalities. There has been more concern with developing basic skills from which couples could create-- and continue to create--their own unique interactional patterns which leave room for individual differences. The significance of this encouragement of uniqueness is found in the discussion of Lewis et al. of the characteristics of respectful negotiation:

> Related to the high degrees of closeness apparent in optimal families was the structural characteristic of respectful negotiation. Because separateness with closeness was the family norm, differences were tolerated and conflicts were approached through negotiation which respected the rights of others to feel, perceive, and respond differently. There was not tidal pull toward a family oneness which obliterates individual distinctions.[3]

The workshop begins by presenting the number of channels in which communication can occur between spouses and the importance of nonverbal communication. The communication skills taught are those of listening--attending, observing, paraphrasing, and reaching for information.[4] The negotiation skills taught are those of pinpointing the question, staying with the question, deferring the question,

---

3. Ibid., p. 221.
4. Based on Ruth R. Middleman and Gale Goldberg, <u>Social Service Delivery: A Structural Approach to Social Work Practice</u> (New York: Columbia University Press, 1974), pp. 115-17.

labeling behavior, determining whether the question is one of fact or opinion, and negotiating questions of opinion. Although a number of others have developed similar concepts to those involved in these skills, they have been labeled as negotiation skills by this author.

At this point, there is no way of determining whether the teaching of these skills will indeed develop the three characteristics of interaction on which their formulation is based. The skills themselves have been developed from a variety of sources; they are put together in a systematic way in the anticipation of creating the means whereby the above characteristics of healthy family interaction can be developed. Preworkshop and postworkshop questionnaires can provide some initital indications of whether this is so.

THE FRAME OF REFERENCE[5]

Trainers and Participants

The workshop is designed for use by two leaders, a male and a female. It could, however, be adapted for use by a single leader with some alterations and substitutions of participants in the designed simulations and role plays. The primary reason for the use of two leaders is to provide modeling of specific skills and to demonstrate through the use of role play.

The workshop is best suited to a maximum of ten couples in order to provide for adequate interaction and involvement. As long as there

---

5. Based on Ruth R. Middleman, "Teaching and Training: A Study Guide," mimeographed (Louisville: University of Louisville, 1976).

is an even number of couples, however, the number of participants is flexible and could certainly be increased. It is also ideal if each couple who participates has a long-term commitment to their relationship rather than a question about whether or not to continue it.

Goal Setting

Expectations. The overall educational goals for this workshop are (1) to give information about how to communicate more effectively in marriage and (2) for participants to understand and analyze their own communication patterns and to gain skill in communicating and negotiating more effectively. These goals should be viewed in their relationship to the premises that optimum marital interaction includes: (1) a respect for one's own and the subjective world view of others; (2) openness in communication versus distancing, obscuring, and confusing mechanisms; and (3) spontaneity versus rigid stereotyped interactions.[6] Limitations of time and possible hidden agendas--for example, those coming with "can this marriage be saved?" questions implicit in their participation--necessitate concentration on key skills and as much practice as is feasible.

Specific objectives. Specific goals and training objectives are included at the beginning of each session, along with a brief outline of the activities which will implement those objectives. Although the goals imply the teaching of facts and principles, behaviors, values and attitudes, and dispositions, the manual is explicitly concerned with teaching skills.

---

6. Lewis et al., *No Single Thread*, p. 202.

The process of learning a skill first involves observation, analysis, and then imitation.[7] The exercises planned include opportunities for participants to master the skill at these three levels and to begin to develop some precision in using the skill. There is concern that the participant is provided with the opportunity for identifying the conditions which call for the use of the skill, for understanding the benefits of using the skill, and then for actual practice of the skill. Participants should become familiar enough with the skills that they can continue practice to reach higher levels of precision beyond the framework of the workshop.

How results will be measured. Written tests can assess knowledge about skills and comprehension of when they are appropriately used, but not necessarily ability to apply them. Most appropriate would be an in vivo assessment with rating scales of actual events of marital interaction, but this is usually not possible within the constraints of time and staff. Twice during the sessions participants will rate one another as to the use of skills in role-play situations which will provide some feedback. In addition, questionnaires on which participants will rate themselves and their spouses on the use of the skills are provided to be completed in the first session and one month after the last session. Although this instrument will be too subjective to draw any strong conclusions, it can give a rough measure of the extent to which goals are reached. Copies of the questionnaires can be found in the handout sections of Sessions 1 and 4.

---

7. Ruth R. Middleman, "Heirarchy of Processes for Learning Skills," mimeographed (Louisville: University of Louisville, 1976).

Designing

Organizing ideas. The theoretical basis for the workshop can be found in research on the elements of communication which are found in "optimally functioning" families.[8] The development of these skills cannot adequately be traced to the sources which gave rise to them because they are a compilation of diverse reading which defies foot-noting. Two particularly helpful sources, are the works of Willam J. Lederer and Don D. Jackson[9] and Ruth R. Middleman and Gale Goldberg.[10]

Format. Each of the four sessions is presented in outline form. The first page of the session is a brief outline of what is to be included in the session and the objective of the session. Also, the various activities of the session are listed in order to give an overview and idea of time sequencing. In the following pages, the exercises themselves are in outline form.

The workshop is designed for four sessions lasting from two to two and one-half hours each. If the leaders prefer a more leisurely pace, however, three hours would provide for more interaction and perhaps a midway coffee break.

The actual skills to be covered during the workshop are included in the handout section for Session 1. Xeroxed copies for workshop participants may be helpful, although they may be somewhat overwhelming if given out at the beginning.

---

8. Lewis et al., No Single Thread.
9. William J. Lederer and Don D. Jackson, The Mirages of Marriage (New York: W.W. Norton, 1968).
10. Middleman and Goldberg, Social Service Delivery.

Evaluation

The evaluation instruments detailed above will be used to develop some idea of possible alterations to make the workshop more effective. In addition, time has been allotted for an oral evaluative session at the end of the fourth session to allow the group to make recommendations for future training.

SESSION 1

SESSION 1

BRIEF OUTLINE

OBJECTIVE: To teach the knowledge that communication may occur in a number of channels, that a person cannot not communicate, and that perceptions of the same experience may be quite different. From this knowledge base, to help participants to develop their own guidelines for effective marital communication.

I. INTRODUCTION - GET ACQUAINTED

II. DISTRIBUTION OF PREWORKSHOP QUESTIONNAIRES

III. DISCUSSION OF WORKSHOP

    A. Objectives
    B. Outline of Skills

IV. ROLE PLAYS AND EXERCISES

    A. "A Person Cannot Not Communicate"
    B. Nonverbal Communication
    C. Development of Guidelines for Communication

V. MATERIALS AND HANDOUT SECTION

MATERIALS FOR SESSION 1

    Flipchart or blackboard; feltmarkers or chalk
    Note pads, pens or pencils
    Copies of Preworkshop Questionnaire, pages 29-34
    Outline of Workshop, pages 35-36
    Copies of house diagram, page 41

SESSION 1

In this session, participants will learn to recognize communication problems that are the result of a lack of recognition: (1) that a person is always communicating something and that the message which the sender thinks he is sending is not always the message received, (2) that an incongruity between verbal and nonverbal channels of communication frequently occurs, and (3) that each of several perceptions of the same experience may be equally valid. They will be able to apply this knowledge to actual communication situations by classifying examples of these problems which occur in the structured role play in the session. Accurate classification of one example of each of these problems will indicate successful accomplishment of this session's objective.

I. INTRODUCTION - GET ACQUAINTED

    A. Objective:
        To develop communication between participants and to establish a commitment to the process of the workshop.

    B. Introductions
        1. Leaders
            Leaders introduce themselves by telling a little about themselves.
        2. Participants
            Each participant introduces him or herself to the group. Include name, years married, where from, what they do, and so on.

II. PREWORKSHOP QUESTIONNAIRES

   A. <u>Objective</u>:
      A means of assessing the effectiveness of the workshop.

   B. Preworkshop questionnaires (see Handout Section, pages 29-34) are distributed, and leaders explain that the questions should be answered as honestly as possible.
      The leaders should stress that the questionnaires are intended as an evaluation of the effectiveness of the workshop--not an evaluation of the participants.

   C. After sufficient time has elapsed (about twenty minutes), completed questionnaires are collected by leaders.

III. DISCUSSION OF WORKSHOP

    A. <u>Objectives</u>:

       To provide an opportunity to recognize that the workshop experience may be quite different for different people.
       To define the difference between training and therapy.
       To involve the participants in the process of the workshop.

      1. Leaders explain the basic objectives of the workshop (see pages 35-36 for list of objectives) and introduce the main focus as that of learning more effective communication in marriage.

         Emphasize that this workshop is to be "Skills Training," not therapy, and that the emphasis will be on the "process" of communication rather than the "content."

      2. Leaders ask participants for their specific outcome expectations for the workshop.

         a. List expectations on flipchart or blackboard.

         b. Discuss this list, focusing discussion on the different experiences and expectations which have brought individual participants to the workshop by asking them to look at the responses recorded.

             What can this tell us about how people see things?
             Were some "right" and others "wrong"?
             What can this say about communication in marriage?
             What happens when spouses have different perceptions or expectations of the same experience?
             Is one "right" and the other "wrong"?

         c. Continue discussion until group has selected major

outcome goals on which they wish to focus. (See page 40 for sample list.)

B. <u>Outline of Course Skills</u>

Provide participants with an outline (see handout, pages 37-39) of the skills to be covered in the workshop.

Discuss this outline briefly, relating skills to the outcome goals selected by the participants.

IV. ROLE PLAYS AND EXERCISES

   A. "A Person Cannot Not Communicate"
      1. <u>Objectives</u>: To allow participants to see that a person is always communicating.
         To provide an opportunity for participants to experience awareness that the message sent is not always the message received, and that communication may not be congruent in all channels.
         To provide an opportunity for participants to apply these concepts to marital communication.
      2. <u>Main concepts</u>: A person cannot not communicate. One is able to listen with more awareness of the message of the speaker when he is not preparing a response.
      3. <u>Role play</u>
         a. Leaders ask for a couple to volunteer. They are given written instructions as follows:

         Husband: You are to convince your wife to do something for you that you have wanted to do for a long time but she is not too excited about (for example, go to a baseball game with you, cook a special meal, change her hair color, and so forth). You are to do this without getting her to respond to you--she is being instructed to let you do all the talking and she the listening.
         Wife: Your husband is going to try to convince you to do something special for him. You are not to communicate with him--do not respond in

words, facial expressions, body movements. Try not to communicate in any way.

They are not to share the written instructions with each other or with the group.
  b. Before the role play begins, the leaders instruct the group to observe the process of communication taking place--the attitudes and the feelings expressed.
  c. The couple begin the role play and are stopped by leaders after enough process for discussion has taken place.
  d. Leaders ask the group to discuss what they saw being communicated by the participants. Leaders may need to focus the group on feeling process rather than content.
  e. Leaders ask the couple doing the role play to share their special written instructions with the rest of the group and to express any feelings they had while playing their parts.
4. Discussion
The group examines the messages that were transmitted of which participants were unaware and the implications of this for marital communication. What does this mean in terms of developing more effective communication? Discussion continues until main concepts are induced and processed by the group.

B. Nonverbal Communication
  1. Objectives: To provide an opportunity for participants to see the importance of nonverbal communication in

listening effectively.

To provide an opportunity for generalization of this concept to problems in marital communication.

2. <u>Main concepts</u>: We use many levels of communication when interacting with one another.

At times we send double (incongruent) messages.

3. <u>Exercise</u>
   a. Leaders ask each couple to place their chairs back to back. Be sure that pairs are spaced far enough apart so that there is minimal disruption for other couples.
   b. Each wife is given a house diagram (see page 41) which she is not to show her husband.
   c. Each wife is asked to instruct her husband verbally to draw this diagram. Participants are told that they will have seven minutes to complete this task.
   d. At the end of seven minutes, the leaders reconvene the group and collect the husbands' drawings, which are then displayed to the group.
   e. Leaders ask the group what difficulties they had in completing this task and why.

4. <u>Discussion</u>

   Discuss the importance of nonverbal communication and the implications this has (including incongruent messages) for marital interaction. Discussion ends when main concepts have been induced and processed.

C. <u>Development of Guidelines for Communication</u>

Leaders role play a scene of marital communication, being careful to include incidences of (1) attempts not to communicate (reading a newspaper, not listening, and so forth), (2) incongruent messages, and (3) different perceptions of the same stimulus. The role play situation should be decided on by leaders before the session in order to provide a smooth transition. Participants are instructed to note examples of the three problems discussed.

1. <u>Sample Role Play</u>

    Setting: Husband's parents have just left after Sunday dinner. Husband is reading paper, wife is sitting down, staring at the dirty dishes still on the table.

    Sue: They seemed to enjoy themselves, but I surely am tired. (Sarcastically) Your mother is <u>so</u> helpful to let me do the dishes "my own way."

    Jim: Uhm.

    Sue: Well, I guess I'd better get in there and do them (obviously reluctant and wanting some help).

    Jim: The Dodgers won yesterday.

    Sue: You are so selfish! How can you sit there with your feet up and let me spend the rest of the afternoon with the dishes? You're not even listening to me! All you care about is your old paper.

    Jim: All right, I'll be there in a minute (not moving).

    Sue: (Getting up) You didn't even enjoy your dinner; you think I'll never measure up to your mother's cooking.

    Jim: (Evenly) It was a great dinner. You're twice as good a cook as my mother. The roast was a little too done, though.

Sue: (Trying to hold back anger and remaining silent.)

Jim: Now don't get mad over a silly little roast.

Sue: It's not silly!

Jim: (Muttering) I'm just trying to be helpful (still sitting with newspaper).

Sue: Some help you are!!

2. <u>Discussion</u>

At the end of the role play, participants are asked to share and discuss what they observed. From this discussion and from the concepts discussed previously, they are encouraged to develop together a few brief "Guidelines for Communication" in a brainstorming-type format (without critical comments). These are recorded by one of the leaders for distribution at the second session. (See sample list of "Guidelines for Communication" on page 42.)

HANDOUTS

FOR

SESSION 1

Preworkshop Questionnaire
Communication in Marriage

Please answer this questionnaire as honestly as possible. It is not meant to assess you or your marriage: it is intended to help us know what the interests and concerns are which you bring with you to this workshop.

What is the biggest problem you and your spouse have in communicating with one another?

What do you hope to get out of the workshop?

1.

2.

3.

© 1978 Family Service Association of America

Answer the following questions by putting a slash on the line to indicate your answer.

Example: I enjoy watching TV:

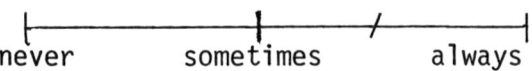

1. When I talk to my spouse, my spouse listens to me:

2. When my spouse talks to me, I listen to my spouse:

3. When I talk to my spouse, my spouse leaves the room or reads the paper:

4. When my spouse talks to me, I leave the room or read the paper:

5. When we argue, my spouse is interested in what I have to say:

6. When we argue, I show my spouse that I am interested in what he/she has to say:

7. When we are discussing something, my spouse shows interest in my viewpoint by asking me to tell more about it:

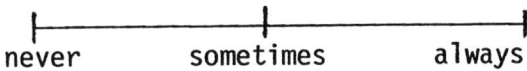

8. When we are discussing something, I show interest in my spouse's viewpoint by asking him/her more about it:

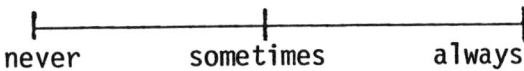

9. My spouse is able to state *my* position in an argument:

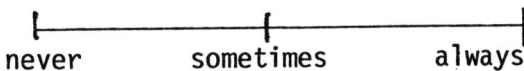

© 1978 Family Service Association of America

10. I am able to state my spouse's position in an argument:

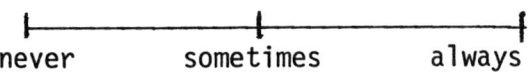

11. My spouse misses the point of what I am trying to say by taking me too literally:

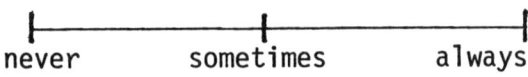

12. I miss the point of what my spouse is trying to say by taking my spouse too literally:

13. We reach some kind of agreement after we argue:

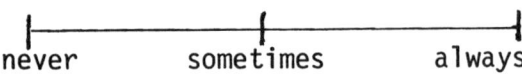

14. When we argue, I know what we are arguing about:

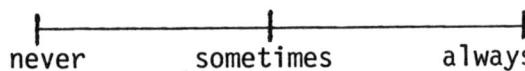

15. When we argue, my spouse knows what we are arguing about:

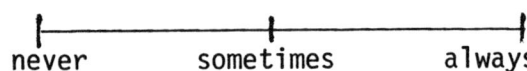

© 1978 Family Service Association of America

16. We argue about issues we have argued about before:

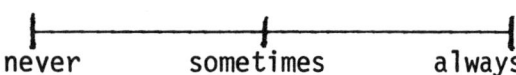

17. The biggest issue in our arguments is who is right and who is wrong:

18. Our arguments are not over who is right or wrong but over opinions we have about things:

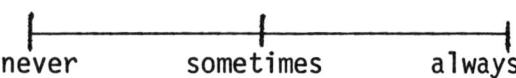

19. My spouse calls me derogatory names:

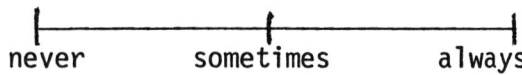

20. I call my spouse derogatory names:

21. My spouse gets out of arguments by refusing to argue:

© 1978 Family Service Association of America

22. I get out of arguments by refusing to argue:

23. My spouse brings up past problems when we argue:

24. I bring up past problems when we argue:

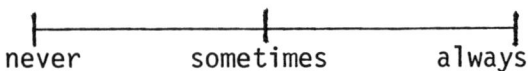

25. My spouse tries to read my mind:

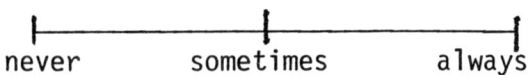

26. My spouse and I see things the same way:

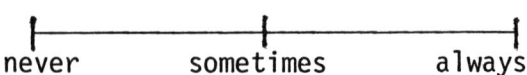

27. My spouse and I communicate in ways other than talking:

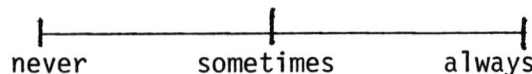

© 1978 Family Service Association of America

OUTLINE OF COURSE

SESSION 1

> OBJECTIVE: To teach the knowledge that communication may occur in a number of channels, that a person cannot not communicate, and that perceptions of the same experience may be quite different. From this knowledge base, to help participants to develop their own guidelines for effective marital communication.

Preworkshop Questionnaire

Discussion of Workshop

Role Plays and Exercises

SESSION 2

> OBJECTIVE: To teach the listening skills of attending, observing, paraphrasing, and reaching for information.

Role Plays and Exercises
    Paraphrasing
    Observing and Attending Skills
    Reaching for Information

SESSION 3

OBJECTIVE: To teach negotiation skills of pinpointing the question, staying with the pinpointed issue, deferring the question, labeling behavior, and determining whether the question is one of fact or opinion.

Role Plays and Exercises
  Pinpointing the Question
  Staying on the Issue
  Determination of Fact or Opinion

SESSION 4

OBJECTIVE: To explore the difficulties in agreeing on matters of fact and in negotiating matters of opinion in marital discussions. To help participants generalize and apply this understanding to their own marital disagreements.

Role Plays and Exercises
  Matters of Fact
  Matters of Opinion

Summary of Workshop

Values Questionnaire

Postworkshop Questionnaire

SKILLS TO BE COVERED IN WORKSHOP

Paraphrasing
    How: Repeating to the speaker in your own words what he said
    When to use: To indicate that you hear and understand what he is saying
                 To check out any inferences you have drawn from what he said

Attending
    How: Orienting body position toward speaker and maintaining eye contact
    When to use: When engaged in a communicative sequence with another person

Observing nonverbal behavior
    How: Call attention to nonverbal behavior
    When to use: When verbal and nonverbal behaviors are incongruent
                 When feelings are not being expressed verbally

Reaching for information
    How: Ask open-ended questions by asking the speaker to elaborate on what he has said
          Ask closed questions by asking for a specific fact
    When to use: You do not understand what is being communicated (open-ended question)
                 You would like to explore an issue further (open-ended question)
                 You are trying to pinpoint an issue (closed question)

© 1978 Family Service Association of America

Pinpointing the question
> How: Ask the following open-ended questions--"What is it that we do not agree on?" "If we agree on a solution to this question, will the same argument occur again?"
> When to use: There is a disagreement about a future behavior or behaviors
> The issue of disagreement has not been clarified

Staying with the pinpointed issue
> How: Restate the question which was pinpointed
> When to use: Past or other issues are communicated

Deferring the question
> How: Agree on a mutually convenient time to discuss the issue
> When to use: An issue has been pinpointed but there is not time to discuss it
> An issue has been pinpointed, but one or both spouses want time to "cool off" and/or think about the issue

Labeling behavior
> How: Point out a specific behavior of your spouse, how it affects you, and how you would like it to be different
> When to use: You want a change in your spouse's behavior

Determining whether the question is one of fact or of opinion
> How: Ask the question, "Is there one answer to this question and all others are wrong, or could there still be disagreement when all available facts are researched?"
> When to use: An issue has been pinpointed
> There is still disagreement

Negotiating questions of opinion
- How: Ask the open-ended question, "Why do we have to agree on this, or do we? If so, what _must_ we agree on?"
State position of what has to be agreed on
Discuss compromises until satisfactory answer is reached
- When to use: Pinpointed question is determined to be one of opinion

© 1978 Family Service Association of America

Examples of Major Outcome Goals

To listen to one another more effectively.

To be able to resolve differences about which we argue, but on which we cannot agree, and which consequently reoccur.

To spend some evenings together doing something important for our marriage, away from the children.

To see if other couples have the same problems we do, and how they resolve them.

To share our thoughts and feelings with one another.

To solve some specific problems.

HOUSE DIAGRAM

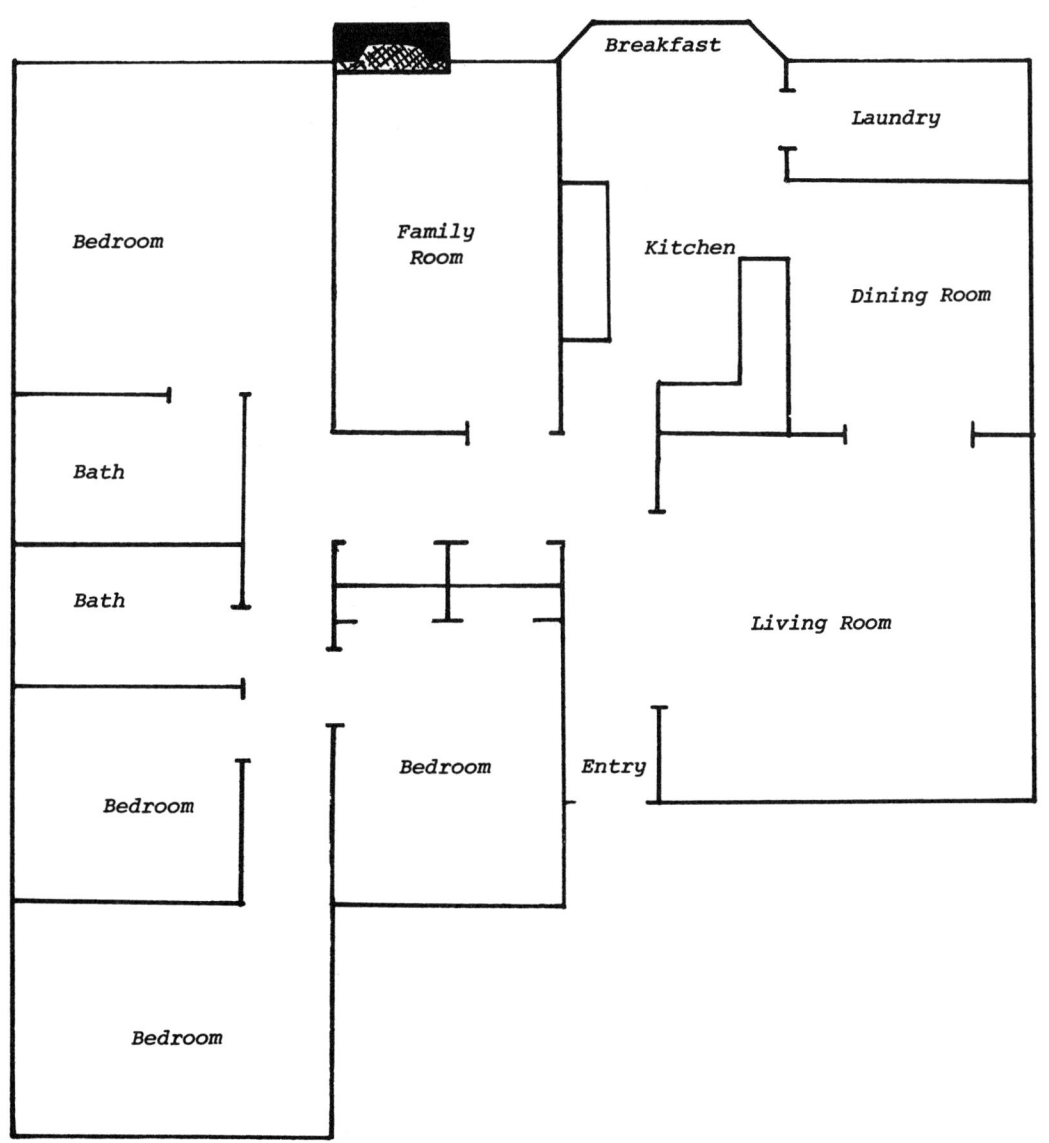

© 1978 Family Service Association of America

Sample
"Guidelines for Communication"

Look at one another when you are conversing.

Recognize that what seems "right" to you may be seen very differently by your partner--and his way may be just as right to him.

When listening to your partner, watch him as well as audibly listening, in order to grasp the full meaning of what he is saying.

Check to see that your partner heard what you meant to say; do not only assume that he did.

Slow down when discussing an issue to allow time to listen to what your partner is saying, then prepare your response.

Tell your partner what you are trying to say nonverbally as well as verbally.

If your partner sends you a double message, point it out and ask for clarification.

© 1978 Family Service Association of America

ADDITIONAL MATERIALS TO BE USED AS HANDOUTS

Brief Outline for Session 1

Instructions to role play on pages 21 and 22

SESSION 2

SESSION 2

BRIEF OUTLINE

OBJECTIVE: To teach the listening skills of attending, observing, paraphrasing, and reaching for information.

I. REVIEW OF SESSION 1

II. OVERVIEW OF SESSION 2

III. ROLE PLAYS AND EXERCISES

    A. Paraphrasing
    B. Observing and Attending Skills
    C. Reaching for Information

IV. SUMMARY OF SESSION 2

V. TOPIC FOR SESSION 3

VI. HANDOUTS

MATERIALS FOR SESSION 2

    Flipchart or blackboard; feltmarkers or chalk
    Note pads, pens or pencils
    Behavior Observation Form I (see page 67)
    Guidelines for Communication (developed in Session 1)

SESSION 2

In this session, participants will learn to identify the skills of attending, observing, paraphrasing, and reaching for information. They will practice these skills in a role-play situation and will be scored by a monitor on their ability to use the skills.

I. REVIEW OF SESSION 1

　　A.　Present a brief review of the three main concepts covered in Session 1 and clarify if necessary.
　　　　1.　"A person cannot not communicate."
　　　　2.　We use many levels of communication--verbal and nonverbal--in interaction with others.
　　　　3.　Different perceptions of the same experience may each be equally valid.

　　B.　Distribute copies of the "Guidelines for Communication" developed in Session 1 and allow time for a brief discussion.

　　C.　Indicate that participants are now ready to put the concepts learned in Session 1 to work in the development of communication skills.

II. OVERVIEW OF SESSION 2

Briefly review the content and format of Session 2, then move directly into the exercises.

III. ROLE PLAYS AND EXERCISES

    A. Paraphrasing

        1. Objectives: To demonstrate the skill of paraphrasing for participants.
To analyze the components of the skill of paraphrasing through discussion.
To practice paraphrasing until participants are able to execute it successfully.
To generalize to the usefulness of paraphrasing in marital interaction.

        2. Main concepts: Listening involves nonverbal as well as verbal channels.
The speaker frequently includes too many ideas which make comprehension difficult.
The listener frequently thinks about what he is going to say rather than what is being said to him.
The essential message may be obscured by paying attention to details or by incongruent messages at different levels.

        3. From the discussion in Session 1 of the problems of understanding and being understood, the leaders move to a discussion of the skill of listening as being basic to communication and the primary skill to be emphasized in this session. The following main points should be covered:

"Listening involves many subskills, one of which is paraphrasing. Paraphrasing is defined as repeating back to the speaker in your own words what he has said in order to indicate that you heard and understand correctly what he has said, or to check out an inference that you have made about what he has said. The speaker will then confirm your accuracy. Paraphrasing involves not only what is said verbally, but also may involve nonverbal behavior. It is an important skill, because so many times we are concentrating on what we are going to say in return rather than paying attention to what is being said to us. It also involves the speaker, who must acknowledge the accuracy of the hearer's perception or correct him."

4. Exercise

   a. The leaders ask for two volunteers (not a married couple) to demonstrate paraphrasing for the group. Have them place their chairs facing one another and give them a topic to discuss (for example, who should handle family finances, whether the husband or the wife should handle the family finances, who should be responsible for writing or communicating on a regular basis with the extended family, how having children can affect a marriage, ways in which couples can decide on which chores each is responsible for). The leaders instruct each volunteer to paraphrase what the other has said before a reply can be given using the following as an example.

   Male: About the finances, well, I take care of them in my family because I am the one working, and I like to see where the money goes.

Female: You are telling me, then, that whoever makes the money ought to be the one to dole it out on bills, and also, that it gives you some enjoyment to know where it is going.

Male: Yes, that is right, but especially the last point. When my wife handled it, I never could quite believe that it took that much to live on, and I kept wondering what she was really doing with the money.

Female: So since you have been handling the finances, you have been more trusting of your wife?

Male: Right! What do you think, from a woman's perspective?

Female: Well, I kind of agree with you on this last part. My husband makes more money than I do, but he does not like to mess with the bills; he always worries about it. But I really get a kick out of getting the bills paid and figuring out how much we can use to do something we really want to.

Male: So you think that whoever enjoys it ought to do it. That is a little different from what I am saying, because you are saying that it does not matter who makes the money. The look on your face makes me think that for you, whoever makes the most money is not an important issue.

Female: Yes, that is about how I feel. You are right, we are different in how we see this.

The leaders should intervene several times during the exercise to see if the speaker is satisfied with the listener's paraphrase. The exercise is continued for five minutes, or until some of the problems of listening are made clear to the rest of the group.

b. At the end of the exercise, the leaders ask the group to formulate suggestions for the speaker and the listener. These suggestions are then recorded on the flipchart or blackboard. They should include derivations of the main concepts noted at the beginning of this exercise.

c. The leaders ask the group to divide into triads, not including the same marital pair in any triad, and to practice paraphrasing, with two of the triad discussing an assigned topic and the third serving as monitor. The monitors are asked to check periodically to see if the discussants are satisfied with the paraphrasing and to give constructive feedback at the end of the practice. Roles are rotated until all have experienced all three roles. Leaders call time every three to five minutes for the purpose of rotating roles. Leaders should move from triad to triad and offer help if necessary.

d. The leaders reconvene the group and elicit an evaluation of the experience and ideas from participants. Applications of paraphrasing to marital interaction are obtained and added to the suggestions already on the board. The questions below (some have been adapted from William Pfeiffer and John E. Jones[1]) may be used for discussion starters:

Was it difficult to paraphrase what the other person said? Why?

When you listened to the speaker, did you forget what you wanted to say?

Did you find that you really do not listen to what is being said?

Did you find yourself preparing your response rather than listening to what was being said?

Was your listener able to paraphrase what you were trying to say to your satisfaction? Why or why not?

Did the speaker use nonverbal behaviors while talking which made it difficult to listen to what he was saying?

How do the ideas that we have generated here apply to the ways in which we listen to and talk to our marital partners?

B. <u>Observing and Attending Skills</u>
   1. <u>Objectives</u>: To provide an explanation of the skills of observing and attending.

---

1. Adapted from William Pfeiffer and John E. Jones, eds., <u>A Handbook of Structured Experiences for Human Relations Training</u>, vol. 1, revised (La Jolla, Calif.: University Associates Press, 1974), p. 35.

To allow participants to see communication difficulties resulting from lack of observing and attending.

To apply the skills of observing and attending to demonstration problems.

2. <u>Main concept</u>: Arguments are frequently sidetracked to issues of process rather than content.

3. The leaders make a brief presentation of the nonverbal aspects of listening and the concepts involved in observing and attending. An example of the presentation follows:

    "Think about the number of messages that are often involved in communication. Did your paraphrasing in the previous exercise involve only the verbal messages? What other messages are involved? In order to listen, one must also be <u>watching</u>, or observing, nonverbal as well as verbal behavior. What kinds of things have you watched for? (Facial expressions, body movements, postures, and so forth.) Think about the times when you think that someone isn't listening to you. What did the receiver <u>do</u> to give you that impression?

    "Attending, or being attentive to what the other person is saying by orienting your body position toward him or her and by maintaining eye contact is of utmost importance in good communication. Observing and attending are two skills which complement paraphrasing in understanding what is being said and in making the speaker feel you are really hearing him or her."

4. <u>Simulated Argument</u>

    a. Leaders ask the group to observe a role play and to watch for "errors" in listening.

b. The two leaders conduct a simulated argument, an example of which follows:

(Jim walks in from work two hours late. As Sue talks to him, he sits down and stares into space.)

Sue: You make me so mad. I have asked you over and over to call if you are going to be late getting home. It's awful to pace the floor not knowing what has happened to you. Dinner's ruined. It's been an awful day; I had a hard day at work, and got in an awful traffic jam coming home, rushed in to fix dinner--and then you don't even show up! (Incredulous) You're not even listening to me!!

Jim: (still staring into space) I heard every word you said--you said dinner's ruined, you had a bad day at work, got stuck in traffic coming home, and you're hot under the collar because you fixed dinner and I didn't make it. Did you ever stop to consider that something might have tied me up so I couldn't call? (Wife crosses her arms and rolls her eyes, turning away from him.) I had an important meeting at 4:00--but never mind, you're not interested.

c. Leaders stop the role play when sufficient communication problems have been presented to support a discussion.

d. The group is then asked how this interaction could

be changed to make it more constructive. Specific suggestions are recorded on the flipchart or blackboard. Interaction is guided to a discussion of how to correct mistakes in communication in process.
    e. The leaders ask one couple to replay the same incident briefly, but correcting the communication errors in line with the group's discussion and recommendations.

C. Reaching for Information
    1. <u>Objectives</u>: To develop verbal guidelines for listening, for example, reaching for information, both with open-ended and closed questions.
       To apply reaching for information in marital discussions.
    2. <u>Main concepts</u>: Reaching for information provides the listener with a better understanding of what is being communicated.
       Reaching for information may express empathy and caring, or at least interest, to the speaker.
       Listening is not only nonverbal behavior but involves active verbal participation in what is being said.
    3. <u>Sample exercise</u>
       The two leaders present a previously rehearsed role play[2] of a marital discussion (for example, where to go on vacation or what happened that day at work). In the role play, one leader expresses his or her feelings about the topic or tells a story about some-

---

2. Adapted from William J. Lederer and Don D. Jackson, <u>The Mirages of Marriage</u> (New York: W.W. Norton, 1968), pp. 283-84.

thing that has happened. The other attempts to interrupt; for example, when the narrator pauses to take a breath or to formulate thoughts, the interrupter quickly makes a comment or asks a question. Also, whenever the narrator uses a word that has more than one meaning, the interrupter shows that he or she assumes the inappropriate meaning is intended. For example:

Jim: Boy, what a day I have had. You would not believe what happened to me today; I . . .

Sue: (Interrupting): It could not compare to this zoo. First the washer overflowed, and, while I was cleaning up the mess, I forgot about my cake, which burned to a crisp before I remembered it.

Jim: Burned is exactly right! I was really burned up when I got to the office this morning and realized that the boss has taken off on a vacation and left a whole pile of stuff for me to do. Sometimes, when I realize that I am doing the work and he is getting the credit, I just feel like quitting.

Sue: But you can't quit, can you? We can't possibly make it on my salary.

Jim: I know, but sometimes I just feel . . .

Sue: I mean, how could we make the house payment, and the car is in bad shape as it is.

Jim: But Sue, I am just so tired of . . .

Sue: (Interrupting) Oh, I know, dear, why don't you just lie down while I get supper on the table?

a. The leaders stop the role play when sufficient incidents have occurred to show how easy it is to make communication difficult.
b. The leaders ask the group what they saw happening. How could the listener have been more effective? What could he have said? Asked? Discussion is guided toward how to question to facilitate discussion and the use of open-ended and closed questions.[3] Group is asked for specific examples from the role play and for more appropriate ways of listening. What is the result of active verbal participation by the listener?
c. Leaders replay the same scene, using open-ended questions appropriately.

Jim: Boy, what a day I have had. You won't believe what happened to me today; I . . .

Sue: (interrupting) I had a bad day, too, but first let me hear about yours. What happened?

Jim: When I got to the office this morning I found out that the boss has taken off on a vacation and left a whole pile of stuff for me to do. Sometimes when I realize that I am doing the work and he is getting the credit, I just feel like quitting.

Sue: You sound so discouraged. Are you serious about quitting?

---

3. For more elaboration, see Ruth R. Middleman and Gale Goldberg, <u>Social Service Delivery: A Structural Approach to Social Work Practice</u> (New York: Columbia University Press, 1974), pp. 115-17.

Jim: Well, yes and no. I have thought about looking for something else.

Sue: That is kind of scary. How would we manage if you quit?

Jim: I don't know, but maybe when I am not so tired we can talk about some possibilities. I appreciate your hearing me out. Now, what happened to you?

Sue: Oh, the washer overflowed and I burned a cake while I was cleaning up the mess . . .

Lead the group to discuss the results of active verbal participation by the listener, as shown in this role play. (For example, the speaker feels he is being listened to, that his ideas are important.)

4. Group Exercise
   a. Participants are asked to divide into triads.
   b. Leaders assign an issue which will elicit some active participation (for example, women's rights). Review the "how" and "when to use" definitions of this skill:

Reaching for information

How: Ask open-ended questions by asking the speaker to elaborate on what he has said, or
Ask closed questions by asking for a specific fact.

When to use: You do not understand what is being communicated (open-ended question), or
You would like to explore an issue further (open-ended question),

        or
   You are trying to pinpoint an issue
   (closed question).
c. Two members of the triad are to practice asking open-ended and closed questions. The third is to act as a monitor, and at the end of the role play to make concrete suggestions to discussants. The monitor is to complete the Behavior Observation Form I (see page 67) which is to be used as the basis of discussion. These forms are collected by the leaders at the end of the exercise and used as part of the workshop evaluation.
d. Participants rotate roles until each has played all three roles.
e. Discussion. The group is reconvened by the leaders who ask for an evaluation of the experience:
   What kinds of problems did you have?
   What was the feeling tone for the participants?
   What do you need to work on?
f. The leaders collect the Behavior Observation Forms.

IV. SUMMARY OF SESSION 2

A. <u>Role Plays and Exercises</u>
Leaders answer any additional questions concerning the material covered in the session.

B. <u>Summary</u>
Summarize the session and briefly review the major concepts and skills. Encourage the group members to practice skills during the week and to bring any questions that they may have to Session 3.

V. TOPIC FOR SESSION 3

Remind the participants that the topic for Session 3 is Negotiation Skills.

Ask the couples to agree, before the next session, on a marital argument that is ongoing, or that has recently occurred, that they would be willing to share with the group for the purpose of working on negotiation skills. This should not be something highly personal or extremely conflictual, but something that they would feel comfortable in sharing.

HANDOUTS
FOR
SESSION 2

Behavior Observation Form I

Please circle the X under the statement that best describes how the person used the skill. This is not a grade of how well he or she did, but of how well we taught that particular skill.

	Needs to review the use of this skill	Used skill at times when it didn't fit	Show knowledge of skill, but did not use when appropriate	Most of time uses appropriately	Uses skills appropriately and with ease
Attending (orienting body position toward speaker and maintaining eye contact)	X	X	X	X	X
Observing (watched nonverbal behavior as well as hearing verbal communication)	X	X	X	X	X
Paraphrasing (repeating to the speaker in own words what he said in order to indicate hearing and understanding)	X	X	X	X	X
Reaching for information with open-ended questions (ask speaker to elaborate)	X	X	X	X	X
Reaching for information with closed questions (ask for specific fact)	X	X	X	X	X

Comments _____

Signature: _____

© 1978 Family Service Association of America

ADDITIONAL MATERIAL TO BE USED AS A HANDOUT

Brief Outline for Session 2

SESSION 3

SESSION 3

BRIEF OUTLINE

OBJECTIVE: To teach negotiation skills of pinpointing the question, staying with the pinpointed issue, deferring the question, labeling behavior, and determining whether the question is one of fact or opinion.

I. REVIEW OF SESSIONS 1 AND 2

II. OVERVIEW OF SESSION 3

III. ROLE PLAYS AND EXERCISES

    A. Pinpointing the Question
    B. Staying on the Issue
    C. Determination of Fact or Opinion

IV. SUMMARY OF SESSION 3

V. HANDOUTS

MATERIALS FOR SESSION 3

    Flipchart or blackboard; feltmarkers or chalk
    Note pads, pens or pencils
    Behavior Observation Form 2, see page 91
    Visual Stimulus picture, see page 89
    True-false quiz, see page 90

SESSION 3

Participants will learn to identify and to apply negotiation skills of pinpointing the question, staying with the pinpointed issue, deferring the question, labeling behavior, and determining whether the question is one of fact or opinion. They will execute these skills in a role-play situation with a monitor, who will score the participants on their ability to meet this objective satisfactorily.

I. REVIEW OF SESSIONS 1 AND 2

Leaders will ask for feedback from the group regarding their application at home of the listening skills covered in the last session. Clarification of questions about the prior material is given at this time. Refer back to the group's goals for the workshop, note the progress already made, and locate where the group is in the process of the workshop.

Leaders may also want to point out that the group will now begin to put to use some of what has been discussed and worked on in the exercises, and that now new skills of negotiation of differences will be learned.

II. OVERVIEW OF SESSION 3

Briefly outline the goals and objectives of Session 3.

III. ROLE PLAYS AND EXERCISES

　　A. Pinpointing the Question
　　　　1. <u>Objectives</u>: To provide information as to how and when to use the skill of pinpointing the question.
　　　　　 To apply the skill of pinpointing the question.
　　　　2. <u>Main concepts</u>: How to handle problems which involve more than one question.
　　　　　 The importance of both members of the pair stating their position as openly as possible in defining a question.
　　　　3. The leaders present the skill of pinpointing the question in a mini-lecture that covers the following points:

　　　　"Frequently, when we argue we get so lost in the process of what is happening and in our emotional reaction to the conflict situation that we lose sight of what started the argument: we may never really figure out what did start it. The first part of an argument, therefore, is a good time to focus on what the conflict is about--or pinpointing the issue. It is important here, as always in communication, to employ the listening skills on which we have already worked. You may pinpoint the question by asking the open-ended question, 'What is it that we don't agree on?' You have pinpointed the question when you can answer 'no' to the following question: 'If we find an answer to this question, will the same argument occur again?' (Write this question on the flipchart or blackboard.) This does not mean that other issues which may be brought up should not be discussed, but they should be tabled for a later time. Discuss one thing at a time. To give you a better feel for this, we are going to enact a marital argument, and we want you to try to pinpoint the question."

4. <u>Sample exercise</u>

Leaders role play a marital argument. This may be of their own design, or the example below:

Joe: I am upset that you gave George enough money to buy a skateboard. He will probably break his neck, but I am even more worried that he thinks money just grows on trees.

Sue: I know, but after all, all the other kids have one.

Joe: You do not understand. He just thinks that all you have to do to get money is to ask Mom.

Sue: He is a typical boy! Why not let him have fun? He will grow up soon enough.

Joe: He is going to grow up a spoiled brat because he always gets what he wants.

Sue: Well, you could set a better example for him, too--and you could start by spending less on your precious golf.

Joe: Golf is important to me! I work long hours to support this family and deserve some fun every once in a while.

Sue: I agree, but the rest of us work hard, too--even the kids have to go to school every day, and we ought to be able to spend some money for fun, too.

Joe: Yeah, but you waste money on some things, like that new sewing machine you never have used.

Sue: I have not had time with everything else I have to do, but I do not see what that has to do with George.

Joe: I just think the whole family is spoiled.

5. <u>Discussion of sample</u>

Leaders discuss the role play with the group and raise the following questions:

What was the real issue?

What happened to it?

Do you think this argument will happen again?

How could it be changed?

Terminate discussion when it becomes clear that the group feels comfortable with their understanding of the situation.

6. <u>Replay of sample</u>
   a. Leaders ask a couple to volunteer to replay the same argument, using the skill of pinpointing the question.
   b. Leaders stop the role play when the question is pinpointed rather than allowing it to continue to solution.

7. Ask the group for feedback and evaluation of the second role play.

B. <u>Staying on the Issue</u>

1. <u>Objectives</u>: To practice the skill of pinpointing the question in "situation plays."

   To explain the skills of staying with the pinpointed

issue, deferring the question, and labeling behavior. To avoid the pitfalls of (1) mind reading, (2) past issues, (3) refusal to discuss, and (4) name-calling. To find examples of problems of staying on the issue in a personal argument and to replay an argument until satisfactorily pinpointing the question, using the above skills.

2. <u>Main concepts</u>: Pinpointing the question is an argument about the argument.

    Pinpointing the question may solve it.

3. Leaders present a mini-lecture on the skills of staying with the pinpointed issue, deferring the question, and labeling behavior, and demonstrating some of the problems which may occur, covering the following points:

    "Many times we don't ever pinpoint the question because we get sidetracked to other things. Now we are going to talk about the skills of staying with the pinpointed issue, deferring the question, and labeling behavior. While talking about the 'dos', we are also going to talk about the 'don'ts'--four of the common ways in which issues get sidetracked.

    "<u>Mind reading</u>. This occurs when we tell another person that we know what he is thinking or feeling. The only way he can respond is to deny it or affirm it, and a denial frequently leads to sidetracking. For example: (Leaders demonstrate)

    (Leader 1) I know what you're thinking. You can't hide it from me. Well, just go ahead and be mad if you want to.

    (Leader 2) I am not mad. But it makes me furious when

>   you think you're so smart.

(Leader 1) You can't deny it. You've been mad all day.

"What makes us think that we can read one another's minds? Nonverbal behavior? Past experience with our spouse? Many times we do get a good perception of what our spouse is thinking, but mind reading is not the best way to bring that out into the open. It is important to say what <u>you</u> are thinking or feeling, not what you think your spouse is. This can be done by using the skill of observing nonverbal behavior.

"Call nonverbal behavior to attention. For example:

>   'You've been awfully quiet all day. It makes me think that you have something on your mind.'

Point out past experiences, either yours or your spouse's. For example:

>   'Last week when you were quiet all day it was because you were angry.'
>
>   or
>
>   'If I had been called what I called you, I would be angry.'"

The leaders then present the following situations to the group and ask for alternatives to handling:

Jim comes in two hours late from work and has not called his wife.

Jim: I'm sorry I'm so late, honey, but I had a big meeting.

Susan: You're always sorry, but that doesn't keep me

     from worrying.
Jim: I just forget to call until I'm already involved in a meeting, and then it's too late.
Susan: Well, you're certainly not upset about it. If you cared about me, you'd remember. You just don't love me anymore.

Bill is sitting with his morning coffee, staring out the window. Mary comes into the kitchen.
Mary: I don't understand you anymore. What have you got to be depressed about on a beautiful morning like this?
Bill: I'm not depressed.
Mary: Yes, you are, or you wouldn't be just sitting there like that.
Bill: I am not, so just pipe down! (Slams out the back door.)

Discuss alternative ways of handling these situations. Ask for volunteer couples to role play them in a more appropriate way.

"Past issues. The only thing we can change is the future. The past, however, influences how we feel and that is why it is important to resolve issues so they don't keep coming up."

Define the skill of staying with the pinpointed issue:
Staying with the pinpointed issue
  How: Restate the question which was pinpointed
  When to use: Past or other issues are communicated
Ask for questions, comments, and examples.

"Refusal to discuss. The neatest way to sidetrack an issue is to refuse to talk about it. There is also a very good chance that the issue will never be resolved. There are times, however, when it may be best to postpone the discussion--not enough time, one or both of you are too angry, or you want to think about it first. If so, agree on a time when you will discuss it; do not let it just drop."

Define the skill of deferring the question:

Deferring the question

 How: Agree on a mutually convenient time to discuss the issue

 When to use: An issue has been pinpointed but there is not time to discuss it, or an issue has been pinpointed but one or both want time to "cool off" and think about the issue

Ask for questions, comments, and examples.

"Name calling. Calling your spouse a derogatory name is a good way to escalate emotions in a discussion and to sidetrack onto a discussion of personalities rather than the issues. What is the behavior that makes the name appropriate in your mind? Use the skill of labeling behavior appropriately.

For example, 'You are such a nag.'
 Instead:
  'It really annoys me when you raise your voice and yell like that.'

"That behavior may be the issue, or an issue you will want to talk about at another time if you are already discussing an issue."

Ask for questions, comments, and examples.

4. <u>Pinpointing the Question Exercise</u>
   a. Leaders ask couples to form groups of four.
   b. One couple in each small group then "situation plays" an argument they previously agreed upon during the week, and the other couple points out "sidetracks." <u>It should be emphasized that the goal is to pinpoint the issue, not resolve it.</u>
   c. The couple then replays the argument, using new skills, until they are able to pinpoint the question.
   d. The second couple is asked to complete Behavior Observation Form 2 (see page 91) during the replay and discuss any problems with the situation-playing couple.
   e. Roles are then reversed and the other couple completes the procedure.

5. <u>Discussion</u>
   Leaders reconvene the whole group and ask for feedback. If any group was unable to pinpoint the question, this is brought to the attention of the total group for help. Role-play situations are evaluated and discussed.

C. <u>Determination of Fact or Opinion</u>
   1. <u>Objectives</u>: To see that several perceptions of the same experience are equally valid and valued. To understand the difference between fact and opinion.

To practice the skill of determining whether the question is one of fact or opinion.

2. <u>Main concepts</u>: Perceptions of the same experience are different for different individuals and what may look like a matter of fact is really a matter of opinion.

   Perception is selective.

3. <u>Exercise</u>
   a. Leaders show the stimulus picture (see page 89) to the group. Do not allow them to study it too long.
   b. Have the group complete the True-False quiz (see page 90). Review the answers. When discrepancies occur on questions 5 and 7, leaders should encourage a discussion of who is right and who is wrong. There is both a young and an old woman in the picture; leaders should answer this question in the way opposite the majority to promote discussion.
   c. Show the stimulus picture again and follow it with a discussion as to the different perceptions of the same stimulus and the revelation that there is no right and no wrong. Explore the implications of this for marital communication; for example, what difference does it make whether an argument is about fact or opinion? How would you successfully argue about a question of fact (for example, what week a vacation begins)? The group is led through a discussion to see what is involved in finding the right answer, that is, going to some source which has the answer rather than trying to negotiate a compromise.

And what about questions of opinion? Help the group to see that questions of opinion call for negotiating to find a <u>satisfactory</u> answer, not <u>the</u> answer. This frequently involves compromise.

d. Leaders ask the small groups from the previous exercise, to reconvene briefly to decide whether the questions they had discussed (in the "Pinpointing the Question" exercise) were of fact or opinion. These are to be written on the Behavior Observation Form 2 and brought to the large group. The leaders reconvene the large group and ask how many reached decisions. Discuss those about which there was disagreement. What kinds of questions were involved? How many issues were fact-related, and how many were opinion-related? Continue the discussion until there is a general understanding of the issues involved.

IV. SUMMARY OF SESSION 3

Leaders summarize session and inform the group that they will be coming back to these same kinds of questions next week.

HANDOUTS

FOR

SESSION 3

This illustration of E. G. Boring's "A New Ambiguous Figure" is taken from J. D. Ingalls, <u>A Trainers Guide to Andragogy</u>, Department of Health, Education, and Welfare (Washington, D.C.: U. S. Government Printing Office, March 1972).

True-False Quiz*

Circle the correct answer

1. It is a picture of a lady.   T   F

2. She has a fur around her neck.   T   F

3. The feather in her hair is curved.   T   F

4. The cloth piece does not cover the
   front part of her hair.   T   F

5. The lady seems to be rich.   T   F

6. Her hair is dark.   T   F

7. She is probably 30 years old or
   younger.   T   F

---

*True-False Quiz was adapted from Donald Nylen, J. Robert Mitchell, and Anthony Stout, <u>Handbook of Staff Development and Human Relations Training: Materials Developed for Use in Africa</u> (Washington, D.C.: National Training Laboratories for Applied Behavioral Science, 1967), p. 124.

© 1978 Family Service Association of America

Behavior Observation
Form 2

In the second role play, indicate how many times the person behaved in the following ways by placing + after the behavior. Place - for the "not" behaviors.

Observing nonverbal behavior_____
    (not mind-reading)

Staying with the pinpointed issue_____
    (not bringing up past issues)

Deferring the question_____
    (not refusal to discuss the issue)

Labeling behavior_____
    (not name-calling)

****

Was this couple able to pinpoint the question?_____

What was it?_____

                                Signature_____

ADDITIONAL MATERIAL   TO BE USED AS HANDOUT

Brief Outline of Session 3

SESSION 4

SESSION 4

BRIEF OUTLINE

OBJECTIVE: To explore the difficulties in agreeing on matters of fact and in negotiating matters of opinion in marital discussions.
To help participants to generalize and apply this understanding to their own marital disagreements.

I. REVIEW OF SESSION 3

II. OVERVIEW OF SESSION 4

III. ROLE PLAYS AND EXERCISES

    A. Matters of Fact
        1. Objective
        2. Broken Squares Exercise

    B. Matters of Opinion
        1. Objectives
        2. Mini-lecture
        3. Value Questionnaire
        4. Exercise

IV. SUMMARY OF WORKSHOP

V. HANDOUTS

MATERIALS FOR SESSION 4

    Flipchart or blackboard; feltmarkers or chalk
    Pencils or pens
    "Broken Square" packets (see page 107)
    Values Questionnaire (see pages 108-11)
    List of goals from Session 1

SESSION 4

The participants will be aware of the problems they experience in discussions in which the goal is agreement on matters of fact and in discussions in which the goal is a negotiated solution of differences in matters of opinion. This awareness will be indicated through group discussion and through the development of individual tasks to increase negotiation skills, which will be recorded in writing.

I. REVIEW OF SESSION 3

Leaders summarize and review the material covered in Session 3. Ask the group for comments, questions, and evaluations. Clarify if necessary.

II. OVERVIEW OF SESSION 4

This session is to be spent looking at some of the problems experienced in marriage when the spouses cannot agree on matters of fact or on matters of opinion. By the end of this session, participants should have incorporated the skills learned in the past sessions and will have developed their own goals for increasing their skill in negotiating conflict.

III. ROLE PLAYS AND EXERCISES

   A. <u>Matters of Fact</u>[1]
      1. <u>Objectives</u>: To analyze some of the problems in reaching
         <u>the</u> answer when the question is one of fact.
         To sensitize members to some of their own behaviors
         which may help or hinder this process.
      2. <u>Main concepts</u>: Reaching agreement about a matter of
         fact involves a number of problems which may hinder
         solution.
         There is a need for each individual to understand the
         question.
         There is a need to define how each individual can help
         in solving the problem.
         Each individual needs to be aware of the potential
         helpfulness of the other in solving the problem rather
         than seeing him or her as a mind to be changed.
         There is a need to be aware of the other's viewpoint.
      3. Broken Squares Exercise
         a. The leaders ask the group to form small groups of
            two couples each. One member in each group is
            given a large envelope with four packets inside
            (see page 107). Each member of the group is
            given one packet.

---

1. Adapted from Donald Nylen, J. Robert Mitchell, and Anthony Stout, <u>Handbook of Development and Human Relations Training: Materials Developed for Use in Africa</u> (Washington, D.C.: National Training Laboratories for Applied Behavioral Science, 1967), pp. 143-46.

<u>The packets are not to be opened until the leaders have completed giving the instructions.</u>

b. Read the instructions to the group:
"You each have an envelope which has pieces of cardboard for forming squares. When I tell you to begin, your group is to form four squares of equal size. The task is complete when each individual has a perfect square of the same size as that held by the others in his or her group. There is one rule--no member may speak or signal to another group member."

c. When several groups have completed their squares, the leaders call time and discuss the experience. Some important questions to cover are:
> How did you feel when someone holding a key piece did not see the solution?
> How did you feel when someone had completed his square incorrectly and then sat back with a self-satisfied smile?
> What feelings did you think he or she had?
> How did you feel about the person who could not see the solution as quickly as others could?
> Did you want to help?

d. Relate this discussion to marital arguments over facts.
> How do you feel when your spouse thinks he or she knows the answer and is wrong, at least in your mind?
> How do you, and can you, go about reaching

agreement?

What can you change in your own behavior to be more effective?

B. <u>Matters of Opinion</u>
   1. <u>Objectives</u>: To provide an explanation of the skill of negotiating matters of opinion.
      To explore the differences in opinion which create marital arguments.
      To negotiate a difference of opinion successfully.
   2. <u>Main concept</u>: Acceptance of individual differences allows for individual and marital "growth."
   3. The leaders present a mini-lecture on the skill of negotiating matters of opinion. The following main points should be included:

"In negotiating matters of opinion, it is not a matter of right or wrong, but on what you can agree. The first question which must be answered is, Why do we have to agree on this, or do we have to agree? Can we agree to disagree? If not, on what <u>must</u> we agree? How strongly do we each feel about our positions? Who is most affected? Can we make a swap of some kind?"

The leaders role play this kind of difference, using the situation posed in the role play in Session 3 (see pages 76-77).

At the end of the role play, point out that it is helpful to be tuned in to what some of the differences of opinion are which may cause conflict.

4. Ask each individual to complete the Values Questionnaire. (See pages 108-11.)
   Point out that there are no right or wrong answers.
5. <u>Group Exercise</u>
   a. The group breaks into groups of four used in the previous exercise. Spouses should compare their questionnaires and then pick a topic which seems to create a conflict for them.
      Using all the skills learned during the workshop, they are to negotiate for agreement, or to agree to disagree, with the other couple serving as monitors. The other couple then does the same.
   b. While participants are in the small groups, the leaders ask each individual, with the help of his or her group, to develop a task to increase his or her skill in negotiating conflict. This may stem either from this exercise or from the previous one. For example:
      "To ask my wife what her opinion is before telling her she is wrong if she doesn't agree with me. Before assuming that we have to agree on something, I will ask the question why do we have to agree."
   c. The large group is reconvened and asked for feedback and discussion. What problems were experienced?
      If there is time, ask individuals to share their tasks with the larger group.

IV. SUMMARY OF WORKSHOP

A. The leaders summarize what has been covered during the workshop and ask for criticisms and suggestions. Review the goals set during the first session. Were they met? If not, why not? Is the group satisfied? What more would they have liked to learn? What about process? What about the way the content was presented? Was there enough interaction in the group? Too much? Encourage all criticisms or comments.

B. <u>Postworkshop Questionnaire</u>
Tell the group that postworkshop questionnaires will be mailed to them in one month. These are to be completed as honestly as possible in order to provide further feedback data. Remind them that this questionnaire is important because it will indicate what parts of the workshop are most helpful to participants and what needs to be changed.

HANDOUTS
FOR
SESSION 4

Directions for Making a Set of Squares[2]

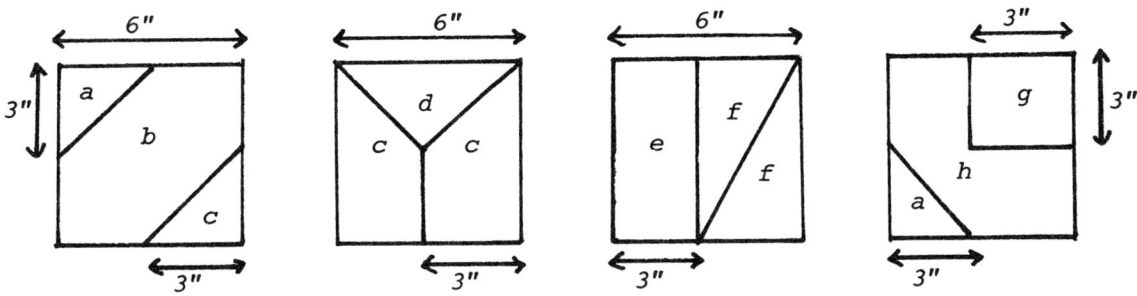

One set of squares should be provided for each group of two couples. A set consists of four envelopes containing pieces of cardboard which have been cut into different patterns and which, when properly arranged, will form four squares of equal size. To prepare a set, cut four cardboard squares of equal size, six by six inches. Mark them as above. The lines should be drawn so that when cut out, all pieces marked "a" will be the same size, all "b" pieces will be the same size, and so forth. By using multiples of three inches, several combinations will be possible that will enable participants to form one or two squares, but only one combination is possible that will form four squares each six by six inches.

After drawing the lines on the squares, cut each square as marked into smaller pieces to make the parts of the puzzle. Mark each of the four envelopes A, B, C, and D. Envelope A contains pieces h, e; envelope B pieces a, a, c; envelope C pieces a, g, c; and envelope D pieces d, f, f, b. Distribute the four envelopes and proceed as described in the exercise.

---

2. Adapted from Nylen et al., Handbook of Development and Human Relations Training, pp. 145-46.

© 1978 Family Service Association of America

VALUES QUESTIONNAIRE

A. Write brief answers to the following questions, then go back and answer them as you think your spouse would. Remember, there are no right or wrong answers.

1. Do you enjoy spending time with friends without your spouse?
2. Who should discipline children in your family?
3. Do you like to drive a big car that has all the extras?
4. Do you enjoy traveling across country?
5. What kind of vacations do you like?
6. Who should be responsible for household chores?
7. Do you enjoy spending time alone?
8. Are you an early riser or a late night person?
9. Is the top of your desk or bureau always cleaned off, or do you usually leave things a little cluttered?
10. Should family members be expected to account for the money they spend?
11. What goals do you hope to achieve in the next ten years?
12. How old should children be before they are allowed to date?
13. How often do you like to visit with your parents? Your in-laws?
14. Are you always on time?
15. What is something you would like to buy but have felt you could not afford?

© 1978 Family Service Association of America

B. A number of activities are listed below. Circle the five which you enjoy most. Then put + through those five you think your spouse likes most. Next, put a check in front of the five you like least, and, finally, put a check behind the five your spouse likes least.

ballet
spectator sports (football, baseball, etc.)
playing active sports
camping
backpacking
canoeing
reading
gardening
entertaining friends
refinishing furniture
traveling
concerts
movies
dining out
bowling
picnics
visiting family

playing cards and games
club or organizational activities
watching television
cooking
creative arts (writing, painting, etc.)
work-related activities
nightclubbing
dancing
political activities
going to museums
shopping
woodworking
working on the car
other (name)_____

C. Circle the answer which most fits you, and check the one which most fits your spouse. Again, remember that there are no right answers.

If I did not care what other people thought and what I might think of myself, I might follow my impulse to:
1. go back to school
2. buy a motorbike
3. learn to ski
4. take a trip around the world
5. write a book
6. buy a farm
7. backpack across the country
8. start a new career
9. join a commune
10. have a baby
11. learn to play an instrument
12. rebuild an engine
13. design and build our own home

I really get angry when:
1. I have to wait for someone who is twenty minutes late.
2. Somebody passes me on the road when I am going the speed limit.
3. Somebody drives the speed limit in the fast lane.
4. The corners of the pages in a book I have loaned to someone have been turned down.
5. My mail has been opened.
6. There is no pencil by the phone.
7. People do not put things away when they are finished with them.

© 1978 Family Service Association of America

8. The car will not run.
9. I am ready to go and a button pops off.
10. I cannot find the car keys.

If I could lead two lives, in my other life I would like to be:
1. a concert pianist
2. a doctor
3. a star football player
4. a train conductor
5. a policeman
6. a fireman
7. President of the United States
8. a writer
9. a cowboy
10. an explorer
11. an astronaut
12. a religious leader
13. a revolutionary

ADDITIONAL MATERIALS TO BE USED AS HANDOUTS

    Brief Outline of Session 4

    List of goals developed from Session 1

Postworkshop Questionnaire
Communication in Marriage

It has been one month since the last workshop session. In order to help us improve our workshop in the future, we need feedback from you as to what was helpful, what was not helpful, and how effective you feel that you and your spouse are in your communication at present. Please answer this questionnaire as honestly as you can.

Was the workshop useful? How?

If we were going to change everything about the workshop but one thing, what should that one thing be?

If we were going to change only one thing, what should it be?

Is there anything you think we should have covered that we didn't? If so, what?

Have you been able to use what you learned? How? If not, why not?

What suggestions or comments do you have about the workshop in general--content covered, number of participants, length and number of sessions, and so forth.

Answer the following questions by putting a slash on the line to indicate your answer.

Example: I enjoy watching TV:

1. When I talk to my spouse, my spouse listens to me:

2. When my spouse talks to me, I listen to my spouse:

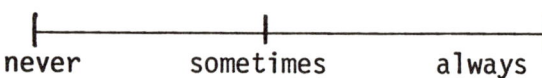

3. When I talk to my spouse, my spouse leaves the room or reads the paper:

4. When my spouse talks to me, I leave the room or read the paper:

            |————————|————————|
            never   sometimes   always

© 1978 Family Service Association of America

5. When we argue, my spouse is interested in what I have to say:

6. When we argue, I show my spouse that I am interested in what he/she has to say:

7. When we are discussing something, my spouse shows interest in my viewpoint by asking me to tell more about it:

8. When we are discussing something, I show interest in my spouse's viewpoint by asking him/her more about it:

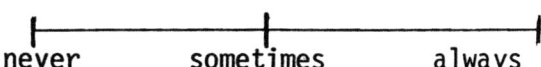

9. My spouse is able to state _my_ position in an argument:

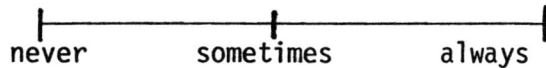

10. I am able to state my spouse's position in an argument:

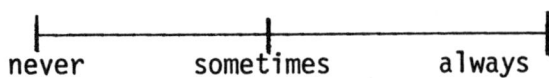

11. My spouse misses the point of what I am trying to say by taking me too literally:

12. I miss the point of what my spouse is trying to say by taking my spouse too literally:

13. We reach some kind of agreement after we argue:

14. When we argue, I know what we are arguing about:

15. When we argue, my spouse knows what we are arguing about:

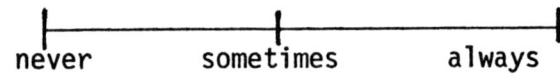

© 1978 Family Service Association of America

16. We argue about issues we have argued about before:

17. The biggest issue in our arguments is who is right and who is wrong:

18. Our arguments are not over who is right or wrong but over opinions we have about things:

19. My spouse calls me derogatory names:

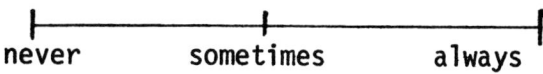

20. I call my spouse derogatory names:

21. My spouse gets out of arguments by refusing to argue:

22. I get out of arguments by refusing to argue:

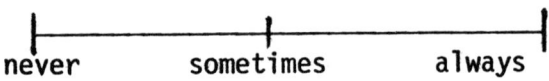

23. My spouse brings up past problems when we argue:

24. I bring up past problems when we argue:

25. My spouse tries to read my mind:

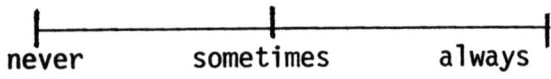

26. My spouse and I see things the same way:

27. My spouse and I communicate in ways other than talking:

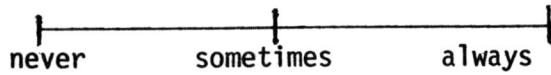

BIBLIOGRAPHY

BIBLIOGRAPHY

Lederer, William J., and Jackson, Don D. *The Mirages of Marriage.* New York: W.W. Norton, 1968.

Lewis, Jerry M.; Beavers, W. Robert; Gossett, John T.; and Phillips, Virginia Austin. *No Single Thread.* New York: Brunner/Mazel, 1976.

Middleman, Ruth R. "Hierarchy of Processes for Learning Skills." Mimeographed. Louisville: University of Louisville, 1976.

_____. "Teaching and Training: A Study Guide." Mimeographed. Louisville: University of Louisville, 1976.

_____, and Goldberg, Gale. *Social Service Delivery: A Structural Approach to Social Work Practice.* New York: Columbia University Press, 1974.

Nylen, Donald; Mitchell, Robert J.; and Stout, Anthony. *Handbook of Staff Development and Human Relations Training: Materials Developed for Use in Africa.* Washington, D.C.: National Training Laboratories for Applied Behavioral Science, 1967.

Pfeiffer, J. William, and Jones, John E. *A Handbook of Structured Experiences for Human Relations Training,* vol. 1, revised. LaJolla, California: University Associates, 1974.